A CourseGuide for

Apologetics at the Cross

Joshua D. Chatraw
and Mark D. Allen

ZONDERVAN
ACADEMIC

ZONDERVAN ACADEMIC

A CourseGuide for Apologetics at the Cross

Copyright © 2019 by Zondervan

ISBN 978-0-310-11086-6 (softcover)

Requests for information should be addressed to:
Zondervan, *3900 Sparks Dr. SE, Grand Rapids, Michigan 49546*

Printed in the United States of America

CONTENTS

Introduction

Welcome to *A CourseGuide for Apologetics at the Cross*. These guides were created for formal and informal students alike who want to engage deeper in biblical, theological, or ministry studies. We hope this guide will provide an opportunity for you to grow not only in your understanding, but also in your faith.

How to Use This Guide

This guide is meant to be used in conjunction with the book *Apologetics at the Cross* and its corresponding videos, *Apologetics at the Cross Video Lectures*. After you have read each chapter in the book and watched the accompanying video lesson, the materials in this guide will help you review and assess what you have learned. Application-oriented questions are included as well.

Each CourseGuide has been individually designed to best equip you in your studies, but in general, you can expect the following components. Most CourseGuides begin every chapter with a "You Should Know" section, which highlights key terminology, people, and facts to remember. This section serves as a helpful summary for directing your studies. Reflection questions, typically two to three per chapter, prompt you to summarize key points you've learned. Discussion questions invite you to an even deeper level of engagement. Finally, most chapters will end with a short quiz to test your retention. You can find the answer key to each quiz at the bottom of the page following it.

For Further Study

CourseGuides accompany books and videos from some of the world's top biblical and theological scholars. They may be used independently, or in small groups or classrooms, offering quality instruction to equip students for academic and ministry pursuits. If you would like to engage in further study with Zondervan's CourseGuides, the full lineup may be viewed online. After completing your studies with *A CourseGuide for Apologetics at the Cross*, we recommend moving on to *A CourseGuide for Evangelism in a Skeptical World* and *A CourseGuide for Cultural Apologetics*.

CHAPTER 1

Apologetics in the Bible (Part 1)

You Should Know

- First Corinthians 2:1–5, upon closer examination, does not speak against apologetics; rather, Paul enhances the biblical mandate of apologetics by demonstrating how to be effectively cultural and contextual.

- Having "cross-colored lenses" is a vital foundation for apologetics; therefore, it is important to examine the many types of apologetic instances in the Bible.

- The heavens act as an apologist for God (Ps. 19; Rom. 1).

- OT prophets often used apologetics in a polemical way, speaking against false gods and proclaiming the God of the Bible as the one true God.

- Miracles and acts of power are used all throughout Scripture by God through the prophets and apostles to demonstrate his power and validate his existence and superiority.

- Jesus performed miracles to validate his message of divinity and of the kingdom of God.

- The Bible is full of evidence in which people can enhance their faith and trust.

- The lives of Jesus Christ's followers ought to have an apologetic impact.

- Sophists: rhetoricians who maintained public careers based on their ability to speak and follow oratorical conventions

- Fulfilled prophecy: employed to persuade unbelieving Jews and to edify those who already believed

Reflection Questions

1. Explain 1 Corinthians 2:1–5 in light of the sophism of Paul's day. What kind of persuasion is this passage shunning?

2. How does God reveal his existence through his care of the world and the people in it? How about through his provision for Israel?

3. How does eyewitness testimony act as an apologetic?

Discussion Question

1. Summarize how creation, general revelation, and providential care demonstrate that God and his creation are apologists.

Quiz

1. (T/F) It's not persuasion that Paul shuns in 1 Corinthians 2, but rather a certain type of manipulative persuasion.

2. _____ were rhetoricians who maintained public careers based on their ability to speak and follow oratorical convention.
   - a) Sophists
   - b) Philosophers
   - c) Senators
   - d) Stoics

3. The goal of apologetics must be _____.
   - a) The cross
   - b) Persuasion

    c) Defense of theism

    d) Intellectual respectability

4. (T/F) Apologetics inevitably goes wrong when it relies on a system, a rhetorical style, or a charismatic personality rather than on the power of the Spirit.

5. A biblical proof text for general revelation is _____.

    a) Psalm 119:1–6

    b) Psalm 18:1–6

    c) Psalm 19:1–6

    d) Psalm 1:1–6

6. The Old Testament prophets spoke:

    a) Ex cathedra

    b) Because of, with, and for their contemporary culture

    c) In favor of, with, and for their contemporary culture

    d) Against, with, and for their contemporary culture

7. Old Testament prophets often challenged their culture in the form of _____.

    a) Polemics

    b) Apologetics

    c) Philosophy

    d) Persuasion

8. Which of the following is NOT one of the differences between biblical cosmology (how the world was formed) and the prevailing cosmological narratives of the ancient Near East (e.g., Enuma Elish)?

    a) God created the world out of a cosmic battle

    b) There is only one God

    c) God is before and above creation

    d) People are created in the image of God to rule creation

9. (T/F) In both testaments, polemic is used as a culturally relevant defense of the true Creator and Redeemer against false gods.

10. Which is NOT a factor cited by Luke in his Gospel and Acts for his nuanced view of the relationship of Jesus and his disciples to the Roman government? (pp. 62–3)
   a) Christians were not a political threat to Rome
   b) The Romans crucified Jesus and imprisoned Paul
   c) Christianity is a revolutionary movement
   d) Christianity transforms people's lives

CHAPTER 2

Apologetics in the Bible (Part 2)

You Should Know

- There is no one specific "biblical apologetic"; rather, there are many types because the biblical authors, under God's inspiration, were contextual and their persuasive arguments were geared towards the culture(s) they were engaging.

- *Personal*, *Ecclesial*, and *Holy Spirit* witness are all forms of agential apologetics.

- Questions are often used as a way to disarm beliefs.

- The Bible answers objections often and does so by anticipating them and/or reframing the objection.

- The Bible provides us with reasons for our suffering and provides the ultimate solution to suffering—Jesus Christ.

- Apologetics in the Bible uses reason and logic in the situatedness of the culture.

- Apocalyptic literature serves as an apologetic tool by showing us an unseen reality and providing hope to suffering communities.

- In some instances, pagan sources are used as an apologetic tool against the culture that employs those sources.

- Storytelling as an apologetic category shows how Christianity tells the best story about reality.

- The grand narrative of the Bible: creation; fall; redemption; new creation

Reflection Questions

1. Should we expect to find a definitive approach to apologetics in the Bible? Why or why not?

2. Explain the three reasons why apologists must keep a balanced perspective about the limits of reason.

3. What is the "big story" of the Bible, and what are its four movements?

Discussion Question

1. What are the three distinct but related apologetic agents in the Bible, and what roles do they play? Explain and summarize them.

Quiz

1. (T/F) We should expect to find a definitive approach to apologetics in the Bible.

2. Which of the following is NOT one of the biblical apologetic agents discussed in this section?
    a) The individual person
    b) The church
    c) Jesus Christ
    d) The Holy Spirit

3. In ancient Near Eastern culture, it was believed that a(n) _____ of something contained the essence of whatever it represented.
    a) Image
    b) Idol
    c) Picture
    d) Representation

4. The apologetic function of _____ is to show how everyday life works best with God at the center.
    a) Image
    b) The church

    c) The Holy Spirit

    d) Wisdom literature

5. Which book of the Bible demonstrates that the expansion of the church was the providential work of God?

    a) Acts

    b) Luke

    c) 1 Corinthians

    d) 1 Peter

6. Which church, through its good works produced by faith, its labor prompted by love, and its endurance inspired by hope in Jesus Christ, witnessed to the vitality of the gospel?

    a) Thessalonian

    b) Corinthian

    c) Ephesian

    d) Roman

7. Which agent plays an active role in helping us to receive and understand the gospel?

    a) God the Father

    b) The church

    c) The Holy Spirit

    d) Jesus Christ

8. (T/F) In the Bible, God often uses a subversive methodology in which he asks insightful questions in order to challenge and undermine false beliefs.

9. (T/F) The Bible uses the genre of wisdom literature as an apologetic method for addressing the problem of suffering.

10. Which is a biblical reason for why people suffer?

    a) Christians suffer because they are lazy

    b) Humanity suffers because of sin

    c) Pain is a part of life

    d) Life is unfair

ANSWER KEY

1. F, 2. C, 3. A, 4. D, 5. A, 6. A, 7. C, 8. T, 9. F, 10. B

CHAPTER 3

Apologetics within the Great Tradition (Part 1)

You Should Know

- The early church faced many threatening heresies in those formative years: Gnosticism, Marcionism, Manichaeism, and Arianism.

- The early church fervently responded to the heresies that threatened the church as seen in the works of these church fathers: Irenaeus, Tertullian, Augustine, and Athanasius.

- The Jews had a number of contentions to Christianity and the church fathers responded to them accordingly.

- In the early church period, Greek and Roman challenges came in the form of political and cultural challenges as well as philosophical challenges.

- The church faced a few heretical challenges in the Middles Ages for which the church continued to respond.

- The church also faced significant Jewish and Muslim challenges in the Middle Ages.

- The Middle Age period saw two quite famous Christian thinkers emerge—St. Anselm of Canterbury and St. Thomas Aquinas.

- Justin Martyr's answers to Jewish objections to Christianity: Old Testament prophecies affirm that Jesus is divine and that he is the Messiah; Christians are better able to interpret the Old Testament, because the new covenant has replaced the old; the church is the new Israel.

- Nestorianism: In the incarnation, Jesus maintained not only two natures but also two persons.

- Anselm's ontological argument: God is that than which nothing greater can be conceived. It is greater to exist in reality than to exist only in the mind. Therefore, God must exist in reality.

Reflection Questions

1. Do we have to build our apologetic from the ground up? How does our present context factor into this discussion?

2. Explain Augustine's "subjective and psychological" approach to apologetics.

3. What are Aquinas's five ways to demonstrate God's existence?

Discussion Question

1. Discuss the heresies of the patristic period and the various apologists' responses to them.

Quiz

1. (T/F) We should discard the apologetic foundation the church has laid down.

2. Which heresy taught that spiritual things are good and material things are bad?
   - a) Arianism
   - b) Gnosticism
   - c) Manicheism
   - d) Marcionism

3. Which theologian refuted Arianism?
   - a) Athanasius
   - b) Augustine

c) Irenaeus
d) Tertullian

4. Who wrote Dialogue with Trypho the Jew?
   a) Augustine
   b) Irenaeus
   c) Justin Martyr
   d) Tertullian

5. Who, more than any other apologist of the second century, developed the argument for Christianity from its antiquity?
   a) Aristides
   b) Athenagoras
   c) Tertullian
   d) Theophilus

6. (T/F) One of the philosophical challenges to Christianity during the patristic period was that "pagan religion is necessary for people to flourish."

7. Which apologetic method combined several different pieces of evidence?
   a) Cumulative case
   b) Paradox
   c) Point-by-point refutation
   d) Metaphor

8. Which patristic theologian argued that Greek philosophy and its logos had nothing to do with Christianity?
   a) Chrysostom
   b) Clement of Alexandria
   c) Justin Martyr
   d) Tertullian

9. Who said, "For I do not seek to understand so that I may believe; but I believe so that I may understand"?
   a) Anselm
   b) Aquinas

    c) Athanasius

    d) Augustine

10. Which is not an element of Anselm's ontological argument?

    a) God is by definition that than which nothing greater can be conceived

    b) It is greater to exist in reality than to exist only in the mind

    c) Movement or change has a mover

    d) God must exist in reality

CHAPTER 4

Apologetics within the Great Tradition (Part 2)

You Should Know

- As we travel through church history, we see that whenever times and locations change, effective apologetics adjust to meet new challenges.

- The longevity of any apologetic methodology depends on its grounding in the cross.

- The Protestant Reformation challenged perceived abuses of the Catholic church both doctrinally and in praxis.

- Luther's, Melanchthon's, and Calvin's different views on reason: Luther believed that reason only truly works inside a framework of faith. Melanchthon believed that reason can prepare someone to receive the gospel. Calvin believed that reason without the Spirit's inner witness cannot convince someone of Christianity's credibility.

- The Catholic church responded to the Reformers as well as continued the church's efforts to rebut the challenges of various faiths outside of the church.

- The Enlightenment brought a whole new set of challenges to the Christian faith and apologetics.

- The Enlightenment/modernity paradigm has influenced the Christian apologetic response in both positive and negative ways: positively, the church has to continue to develop, be creative, and contextualize their content and methodology, and negatively, in that sometimes the commitment to contextualization leads to a compromise of the fundamentals of the faith.

- Empiricism: asserts that people must look for truth in demonstrable data discoverable by the five senses rather than in claims to supernatural or miraculous events

- Rationalism: seeks truth with human logic alone, apart from divine revelation

- Presuppositional apologetics: Christianity must be accepted and presupposed before one can believe in it.

Reflection Questions

1. Why is it necessary to keep the cross at the center of our apologetic? How does that look practically?

2. How did Schleiermacher take contextualization to "an extreme"? Summarize and explain it.

3. Summarize Van Til's presuppositional apologetic.

Discussion Question

1. Compare and contrast how Luther, Melanchthon, and Calvin each view the relationship between reason and the gospel.

Quiz

1. (T/F) Martin Luther accepted Aristotelian philosophy without qualification.

2. (T/F) John Calvin believed that reason without the Spirit's inner witness cannot convince someone of Christianity's credibility.

3. Whose summary of thought is as follows: Humans can progress, as long as they are guided solely by their own rational thoughts and individual freedom?

  a) John Locke
  b) David Hume
  c) Immanuel Kant
  d) René Descartes

4. Whose summary of thought is as follows: We can know things only as they appear to us, not as they actually are?

  a) John Locke
  b) David Hume
  c) Immanuel Kant
  d) René Descartes

5. _____ asserts that people must look for truth in demonstrable data discoverable by the five senses rather than in claims to supernatural or miraculous events.

  a) Empiricism
  b) Rationalism
  c) Individualism
  d) Compatibilism

6. Which is NOT a part of Pascal's apologetic methodology?

  a) The wage
  b) Reasons of the heart
  c) The God-shaped vacuum
  d) The reasonableness of the cross

7. Which apologist claimed that our current world is the best of all possible worlds?

  a) William Paley
  b) Gottfried Wilhelm Leibniz
  c) Joseph Butler
  d) Hugo Grotius

8. Who unintentionally engaged in apologetics by formulating a worldview approach to Christianity?

  a) Abraham Kuyper
  b) Benjamin B. Warfield

c) Karl Barth
d) John Henry Newman

9. (T/F) Abraham Kuyper insisted that logical arguments and hard evidence could prove the inerrancy of Scripture to non-Christians.

10. Cornelius Van Til developed _____ apologetics, which asserts that Christianity is the only worldview that can ground knowledge and rational thought.

a) Classical
b) Kuyperian
c) Presuppositional
d) Amyraldian

CHAPTER 5

Making Sense of the Methods

You Should Know

- Because apologetics is practiced by human beings, apologists are often nuanced and do not fit neatly into defined categories; however, there are general categories (methods) that reflect certain commitments regarding apologetics.

- Classical apologetics is known as the "two-step model" because it argues first for a general theism and then argues more specifically for Christian theism.

- Hard classical apologists insist that a logical argument for theism must precede a historical argument for the reliability of Christian truths. Soft classical apologists show openness by not strictly drawing a line between which types of arguments are allowed in each stage of the two-step approach.

- Evidential apologetics is known as the "one-step model" because it starts with historical arguments for the life, death, and resurrection of Jesus.

- Presuppositional apologetics contends with providing evidence to the unbeliever and asserts that unless the truth of Christianity is presupposed there is no possibility of rationality, truth, or proving anything.

- Experiential/Narratival apologetics does not appeal to man's rationality but makes an appeal to the other existential-type experiences of life and how Christianity is the best explanation of that reality.

- Each of these versions have strengths to admire and weaknesses we must be aware of and avoid.

- There are *soft* and *hard* forms of each method which correspond to the apologist and his position relative to the other methods outside his own.

- Classical apologetics: a "two-step approach" argues first for theism in general and then for Christianity as the most reasonable form of theism.

- Reformed epistemology: an approach in which the de jure and the de facto questions are linked

Reflection Questions

1. What are the two steps of classical apologetics? Summarize the potential strengths of classical apologetics.

2. Briefly summarize the potential weaknesses of presuppositional apologetics. What is the relationship between Frame's soft presuppositionalism and individual arguments?

3. Briefly summarize and explain Reformed epistemology.

Discussion Question

1. Summarize the potential weaknesses of evidence-based apologetic approaches. What about the potential strengths and weaknesses of presuppositional apologetics?

Quiz

1. (T/F) Classical apologetics posits that unaided reason can demonstrate the high probability of Christian realities.

2. Which is a potential strength of classical apologetics?

a) It emphasizes the Bible's endorsement of using evidence and logic to persuade
b) It quickly takes others to the evidence for the historical elements of the gospel
c) It has promoted rigorous historical argumentation for Christianity
d) It emphasizes that sin damages the whole person

3. Which is NOT one of the potential weaknesses of evidence-based approaches?

a) They have lacked the ability to effectively transfer their methodology and arguments to a broad audience
b) Ultimately Scripture should assess what makes for a "good" argument
c) They can lack an appreciation for human situatedness
d) They can view humans as primarily thinking beings and singularly focus on persuasion that appeals cerebrally

4. What is another name for persuading by pushing back against the broader framework of rationality and "common sense" assumptions of a given person or community?

a) Soft classical apologetics
b) Hard classical apologetics
c) Thick reasoning
d) Thin reasoning

5. The method of undermining a non-Christian's worldview by demonstrating that without the Christian God, they cannot consistently claim meaning, truth, or logic is called what?

a) The presuppositional argument
b) The transcendental argument
c) The ontological argument
d) The teleological argument

6. (T/F) Soft presuppositionalists maintain that a transcendental argument should be rigidly distinguished from evidence-based arguments.

7. Which is NOT one of the potential strengths of experiential/narratival apologetics?

   a) It emphasizes the importance of human desire and imagination
   b) It emphasizes the importance of the corporate church as a living apologetic
   c) It emphasizes the importance of Scripture
   d) It is concerned with how living in different cultures shapes people's experiences in life

8. Which apologetic uses four human experiences to connect Christian belief with common human experience?

   a) Soft experiential/narratival
   b) Hard experiential/narratival
   c) Soft presuppositional
   d) Hard presuppositional

9. Which apologetic argues that a Christian does not need to "prove" Christianity for belief in Christianity to be considered rational?

   a) Soft presuppositional
   b) Hard experiential/narratival
   c) Cumulative case
   d) Reformed epistemological

10. (T/F) The best apologetic maps are not drawn for "concrete individuals" but for "mankind in the abstract."

ANSWER KEY

1. T, 2. A, 3. A, 4. C, 5. B, 6. F, 7. C, 8. A, 9. D, 10. F

CHAPTER 6

Taking People to the Cross through Word and Deed

You Should Know

- Everything we reflect on in apologetics should be viewed in light of the cross.

- As we take people to the cross in *word* and *deed* the gospel should be reflected in all we do.

- The gospel announces who Jesus is, what Jesus did, and what Jesus secured.

- Christians should be faithful to the gospel message and flexible in the way they present it.

- It would be a mistake to think that apologetics is the same thing as the gospel.

- The use of rational arguments is a tool that the Holy Spirit can use to bring people to Christ.

- Apologetics also includes our *deeds* as a means to help clear the debris in the unbeliever's path.

- Examples of taking people to the cross through word: being faithful to the gospel; being flexible in presenting the gospel; using apologetics as a tool to clear away doubt; recognizing the role of the Holy Spirit in preparing people's hearts to receive the gospel

- One of the earliest creedal statements: "For what I received I passed on to you as of first importance: that Christ died for our sins according to the Scriptures, that he was buried, that he was raised on the third day according to the Scriptures" (1 Corinthians 15:3–4).

- Long-suffering testimony: Widespread confidence and compassion in the face of persecution and trials were among the distinguishing marks of the early church.

Reflection Questions

1. Briefly summarize the relationship between sharing the gospel and apologetics.

2. What are some similarities between Philippians 1:27–30 and 1 Peter 3:15? In what way does Peter give instructions for the manner in which to defend the faith?

3. How did Jesus's teaching ministry demonstrate a genuine concern for the whole person? How does Jesus's care for the whole person affect our apologetic approach?

Discussion Question

1. Summarize the three gospel categories using Paul's "creedal statement" as a guide. Combining your knowledge of these categories with the respective relationships between apologetics and the gospel, and the Holy Spirit and arguments, explain the apologist's obligation to take people to the cross through word.

Quiz

1. Paul states that the events of the gospel all happened "_____."
    a) According to first importance
    b) According to God's grace
    c) According to the Scriptures
    d) According to the love of God

2. The _____ is at the heart of the Christian message.

    a) Ascension

    b) Crucifixion

    c) Incarnation

    d) Resurrection

3. Which is NOT one of this section's gospel foci extracted from 1 Corinthians 15?

    a) The gospel announces who Jesus is

    b) The gospel announces what Jesus did

    c) The gospel is verified by many witnesses

    d) The gospel promises what Jesus secured

4. (T/F) It would be a mistake to think that apologetics is the same thing as the gospel.

5. Which person of the Trinity works in a person to enable them to receive the gospel message?

    a) The Father

    b) The Son

    c) The Holy Spirit

    d) All of the above

6. Our apologetic appeals are most faithful when they are embedded within a corporate witness marked by long-suffering testimony, _____, and holistic service.

    a) Spiritual truth

    b) Personal transformation

    c) Saving grace

    d) Forgiveness

7. (T/F) Widespread confidence and compassion in the face of persecution were among the distinguishing marks of the early church.

8. What term does Kevin Vanhoozer use to describe the knowledge that embodies the wisdom of the cross and is lived out and cultivated through discipleship within the body of Christ?

    a) Christian wisdom
    b) Christian knowledge
    c) Christian philosophy
    d) Christian apologetics

9. Which scriptural passage encourages believers to lead a "quiet life"?

    a) 1 Thessalonians 4:11–12
    b) Ephesians 4:17, 19
    c) Colossians 3:23
    d) 1 Corinthians 15:3–4

10. Matthew 8:16–17 references what Old Testament passage with regard to Jesus's healing ministry?

    a) Isaiah 2:2–3
    b) Isaiah 11:6–8
    c) Isaiah 53:4
    d) Genesis 1:26–28

CHAPTER 7

Cruciform Humility before God and Others

You Should Know

- The cross serves paradoxically as a symbol of both strength and humility.

- Apologists can either engage in an *apologetics of glory* or be an *apologist at the cross*.

- An *apologist at the cross* has a humility before God and others.

- We must avoid the idol of cultural acceptance especially in the areas of ethics and knowledge.

- Deuteronomy 29:29 says that while the Lord has revealed truth to us, he has not revealed all things to us.

- Jesus and Paul provide us with a particular tone for engaging those inside and outside of the faith.

- The book of Proverbs provides us with many practical lessons for engaging others in humility. Apologetic lessons from Proverbs: listen and take others seriously; avoid falsely representing the other side; resist assuming motives

- The reasons why strong empiricism is problematic: it is self-refuting; it is impractical; not all intelligent people reason and interpret data in the same way; all individuals are born with a fallen human nature

- Modernism: a period of thought that began in the early seventeenth century with René Descartes and is commonly associated with his dictum "I think, therefore I am"

- Strong empiricism: One should not accept anything as true unless it is empirically verified or demonstrated logically.

Reflection Questions

1. Contrast apologists of glory with apologists at the cross.

2. Summarize modernism and its impact on discovering truth. Describe modernism's unrealistic expectation and how it affects the Christian worldview. Use Deuteronomy 29:29 in your answer.

3. What is "apologetic triage" and how does priority of need factor in?

Discussion Question

1. Referencing Romans 1:18–32, describe the three ways a recognition of humankind's sinful nature should chasten any overly rationalistic reflexes we may have.

Quiz

1. (T/F) Apologists should seek to persuade others to change their views because they fear others.

2. When relating the Bible's morality to the culture around them, apologists must first reexamine the Bible to make sure they are not just defending the view of their _____.
   a) Tradition
   b) Culture
   c) Church
   d) Family

3. What was the temptation in the Garden of Eden?
   a) To be gods
   b) Wives to rule over their husbands
   c) To have what one cannot have
   d) To be like God and know as he knows

4. (T/F) Being able to give reasons for Christianity does not mean that we will be able to answer every question with certainty and in a way that will satisfy everyone.

5. The term "_____" refers to a period of thought that began in the early seventeenth century with René Descartes and is commonly associated with his dictum "I think, therefore I am."

   a) Strong empiricism
   b) Modernism
   c) Unrealistic expectations
   d) Postmodernism

6. Which is NOT a reason strong empiricism is problematic?

   a) It is self-refuting
   b) It is irrational
   c) Not all intelligent people reason and interpret data in the same way
   d) All individuals are born with a fallen human nature

7. Which is NOT one of Drs. Chatraw and Allen's observations from Romans 1:18–32?

   a) Sin affects our faith
   b) Sin affects our reasoning structures
   c) Sin affects our affections; it misdirects our desires and loves
   d) Sin affects cultural plausibility structures

8. _____ determine both the sort of things we would even consider believing and the beliefs that many in any given culture or subculture take for granted.

   a) Cultural plausibility structures
   b) Cultural probability structures
   c) Cultural possibility structures
   d) Native rationalities

9. According to the book of _____, believing in God means trusting in a personal being who is infinitely wiser and whose ways are beyond our full understanding.

a) Deuteronomy
b) Isaiah
c) Job
d) Romans

10. Which is NOT one of this unit's lessons gleaned from Proverbs?

a) Listen and take others seriously
b) Avoid falsely representing the other side
c) Resist assuming motives
d) Focus on the periphery

CHAPTER 8

Appealing to the Whole Person for the Sake of the Gospel

You Should Know

- The biblical use of the words *heart* and *mind* is quite different than the modernistic use of the terms and reminds us that we are not compartmentalized beings.

- Our apologetic endeavors should appeal to the whole person.

- Human beings are intellectually reflective and moral beings who worship.

- A healthy apologetic method will remember that human beings are thinking, believing, and desiring creatures.

- Sometimes we need to move beyond rational arguments in our apologetic methods and appeal to others through story and imagination.

- Even though human beings are complex we should not neglect reason or providing good reasons to believe Christianity is true.

- Cultural rationality refers to the frameworks assumed by a culture that defines the sort of things those in that culture consider it plausible to believe.

- Basic laws of logic are a necessary condition for rationality; however, they are not a sufficient condition for rationality.

- Basic logic: used in elementary mathematics and in certain assumed rules for communicating and thinking that seem to be universal

- Frameworks of rationality: refers to broader assumed systems of thought linked to specific historical and social locations that people operate under, influencing how they make and receive arguments

Reflection Questions

1. Explain Smith's three anthropological models.

2. Explain how the corporate practices of the church (worship, baptism, and the Lord's Supper) act as visual apologetics for the gospel.

3. Describe the three basics of logic. Explain the difference between basic logic and frameworks of rationality. Describe Drs. Chatraw's and Allen's example of this difference.

Discussion Question

1. Using biblical examples, discuss how stories and imagination can make a point that will capture the hearer's heart. How do propositions relate to this discussion? How are stories a "particularly important avenue" for Christians to challenge how unbelievers view the world?

Quiz

1. (T/F) In biblical usage, the word heart usually refers to all aspects of the human psyche.

2. Which is NOT one of the specific aspects of a theological anthropology?
   a) Humans are moral beings
   b) Humans are beings who worship
   c) Humans are sinful beings
   d) Humans are intellectually reflective beings

3. (T/F) Apologetics is primarily made up of analytical and empirical methods.

4. Which theologian and philosopher emphasizes desires in the Christian life?

   a) Jonathan Edwards
   b) James K. A. Smith
   c) Martin Luther
   d) John Calvin

5. Which is NOT one of Smith's anthropological models?

   a) Human beings are primarily thinkers
   b) Human beings are primarily believers
   c) Human beings are primarily lovers
   d) Human beings are primarily haters

6. What serves as a fruitful analogy that demonstrates the interplay between thinking, believing, and desiring?

   a) Parenthood
   b) Friendship
   c) Marriage
   d) Childhood

7. Which theologian(s) said that the human heart is restless and that it is a "factory of idols"?

   a) Augustine
   b) John Calvin
   c) Martin Luther
   d) Jonathan Edwards
   e) A & B
   f) None of the above

8. (T/F) Scripture is full of encounters in which one person appeals to others' imagination in order to capture their heart.

9. What are broader assumed systems of thought linked to specific historical and social locations that people operate under?

   a) Framework of rationality
   b) Basic logic
   c) Native rationality
   d) Cultural rationality

CHAPTER 9

Contextualization through the Lens of the Cross

You Should Know

- The message of the gospel is true for all people but the message itself was delivered to and revealed in a particular culture.

- Following Paul's lead, apologists are to take their listener seriously and at the same time allow the gospel to set the limits of contextualization.

- Both Peter and Paul contextualized their apologetic approaches based on the group of people they were engaging.

- Not only is making relevance one's ultimate goal a quick way to become irrelevant, but it also debases contextualization.

- In Acts 2, Peter establishes that Jesus has ushered in specific scriptural expectations of the Jewish people for events that would occur at the restoration of the kingdom. He also appeals to an authority relevant to the Jews: the prophetic passages of the Old Testament. Finally, Peter uses language that would have been accepted and understood by his audience.

- In Acts 17, Paul uses one of their own beliefs to demonstrate that God must be independent from his creation. Furthermore, he argues that their claim to intellectual superiority is inconsistent with the uncertainty about the divine that led them to build an altar to an unknown god.

10. Which is NOT one of the basics of logic?

a) Law of identity
b) Law of noncontradiction
c) Law of the excluded middle
d) Law of commutativity of conjunction

- The assumptions and attitudes of the culture we live in orient and shape us so deeply that we usually don't give much thought to them.

- According to Eckhard Schnabel, 1 Corinthians 9:19–23 instructs apologists to take their listener seriously in a fully consistent manner. The gospel, rather than pragmatics, sets the limits of and propels contextualization.

- Cultural plausibility structures: the beliefs we deem plausible because the people around us support them

- Key text for demonstrating contextualization: "I have become all things to all people so that by all possible means I might save some. I do all this for the sake of the gospel, that I may share in its blessings" (1 Corinthians 9:22–23).

Reflection Questions

1. Describe the two important principles derived from 1 Corinthians 9:19–23 that can be applied to apologetics.

2. Name the specific ways Paul built "a bridge" to relate with the Athenians in Acts 17.

3. Do we give much thought to the assumptions and attitudes of our culture? Why or why not? What does Keller's illustration teach us about cultural plausibility structures?

Discussion Question

1. Summarize Paul's three major strategies when talking with the Athenians on Mars Hill. Now, explain how Paul contextualized the gospel message in his defense of Christianity before the Roman authorities.

Quiz

1. Which biblical passage is an important capstone to the previous units in our study of apologetics?

a) 1 Corinthians 2:1–5
b) 1 Corinthians 9:19–23
c) 1 Corinthians 15:3–4
d) 1 Thessalonians 4:11–12

2. Paul is clear that to _____ is not to abandon the gospel.

a) Prioritize
b) Contextualize
c) Categorize
d) Evangelize

3. Which is NOT one of the specific ways in which Peter reaches out to his Jewish audience in Acts 2?

a) Peter relates to his audience's belief in supernatural beings
b) Peter established that Jesus has ushered in specific scriptural expectations of the Jewish people for events that would occur at the restoration of the kingdom
c) Peter appeals to an authority relevant to the Jews: the prophetic passages of the Old Testament
d) Peter uses language that would have been accepted and understood by his Jewish audience

4. Which is NOT one of the events that would occur at the restoration of the Davidic kingdom?

a) Wonders and signs have occurred
b) The Spirit has been poured out
c) A spirit of anti-Christ has entered the world
d) Jesus fits the criteria expected of "the king greater than David" (i.e., the Messiah)

5. Which is NOT one of the ways Paul builds a bridge to relate to his audience in Acts 17?

a) He relates to their love of philosophy
b) He relates to their desire to worship
c) He relates to their sense that they might be missing something
d) He relates to their belief in supernatural beings

6. (T/F) Paul related to the Athenians' belief in a god who is the source of all life in Acts 17.

7. The book of _____ displays the principles of 1 Corinthians 9 in action.

    a) Romans
    b) Luke
    c) John
    d) Acts

8. (T/F) In their speeches, the apostles tailored their presentation of the universal truth of the gospel to a general audience.

9. (T/F) People's assumptions and beliefs are often historically and culturally conditioned.

10. Understanding _____ structures is vital for apologetics.

    a) Basic logic
    b) Rationality
    c) Cultural plausibility
    d) Native plausibility

CHAPTER 10

Preparing to Engage (not Spin) in Late Modernism from the Inside Out

You Should Know

- There are three basic periods in the history of Western culture: premodernism, modernism, late modernism.

- Two influential aspects of late modernism are the immanent frame and the age of the spinmeister.

- Christian apologists have the option of providing a *spin* or a *take*.

- The "Inside Out" model is a method for engaging others in an others-centered way while remaining focused on the gospel.

- Another effective model of engagement is the use of "A" and "B" doctrines in dialogue.

- The Christian story offers the greatest explanatory power for human experience.

Reflection Questions

1. Is the period of time from the middle of the twentieth century to the present best referred to as *postmodernism* or *late modernism*? Why? What is its relationship to modernism?

2. Give an overview of the "age of the spinmeister" and the "PR effect."

How has the culture of "spinning" made us suspicious when anyone attempts to convince us of anything?

3. Explain Tim Keller's approach for transitioning from the inside of an unbeliever's framework to the outside.

Discussion Question

1. Describe the diagnostic questions for engaging inside a non-Christian "take." Now describe the diagnostic questions for moving outside of a non-Christian "take" to Christianity.

Quiz

1. (T/F) In modernism, the ancient sources of wisdom (e.g., the church) were dethroned and individual reason was crowned in their place.

2. Who were two figureheads of modernism?
    a) René Descartes and Immanuel Kant
    b) Immanuel Kant and Richard Rorty
    c) Richard Rorty and René Descartes
    d) Benedict de Spinoza and Immanuel Kant

3. This movement critiqued the Enlightenment's mechanistic flattening out of life by emphasizing emotion, nature, and aesthetics alongside the individual's primacy.
    a) Modernism
    b) Romanticism
    c) Premodernism
    d) Postmodernism

4. (T/F) While aspects of postmodernism have been called into question, key principles of the Enlightenment are still at work and have only intensified.

5. In _____, to assert that you have personal access to Truth is not only intellectually suspect, but it is also morally wrong.

    a) Postmodernism
    b) Premodernism
    c) Late modernism
    d) Modernism

6. (T/F) The late modern response to modernity's quest to obtain certainty through human reason can be viewed as a relief to Christians.

7. Charles Taylor uses the term "_____" to refer to how, in the current cultural context, people view everything in terms of a natural rather than a supernatural order.

    a) Immaterial frame
    b) Imminence frame
    c) Immediate frame
    d) Immanent frame

8. (T/F) The modern social imagination imbedded in our culture works from the assumption that while people can find immanence, there is no transcendence.

9. (T/F) Spin makes entering into sustained mutual dialogue with those who hold different views difficult because it inevitably leads to "conversation-stoppers."

10. What term refers to a frame of reference that the Christian can internalize and apply to a wide array of apologetic situations?

    a) Immanent frame
    b) Building block
    c) Inside out
    d) Outside-looking-in

CHAPTER 11

Engaging in Late Modernism

You Should Know

- There is a strong connection between the immanent frame and modern pluralism.

- The challenge of modern pluralism is met with the opportunity for Christians to be more intentional and sincere about their faith.

- Christianity is exclusive in that the only way to salvation is through Jesus Christ. It is inclusive because it invites people from all tongues, tribes, and nations to believe in the risen Christ.

- An ethic of authenticity pervades the culture in which expressive individualism, being true to oneself, is the highest good.

- Religious lethargy, a natural outworking of the immanent frame, sees people trying to construct their own webs of meaning apart from any transcendent meaning or purpose.

- The therapeutic turn trades sin for sickness, righteousness for good feelings, and the pastor for the psychiatrist.

- Christians must remember that in any fallen culture there will be aspects of Christianity that will seem crazy, foolish, or dangerous. We must remain true to the gospel, which challenges all human cultures at certain points.

- Theological pluralism: All religious traditions describe the same reality and lead their adherents to the same ultimate destination.

- Expressive individualism: Each person has a unique core of feeling and intuition that should unfold or be expressed if individuality is to be realized.

- Self-authorizing morality: holds personal choice as the highest good

Reflection Questions

1. In what way does modern pluralism present not only a challenge, but also an opportunity to strengthen the church?

2. Summarize expressive individualism and self-authorizing morality. How do you engage with someone whose framework grounds freedom and autonomy in an unbiblical, individualistic conception of flourishing?

3. Discuss the "inside" and the "out" of late modernism's high view of human dignity. Describe the "inside" aspect of sin as idolatry.

Discussion Question

1. Using the inside out approach, analyze theological pluralism. Include discussions on religious skepticism and on inclusivity versus exclusivity. Now analyze humanity's search for self-worth. Is this an internal search?

Quiz

1. (T/F) No longer in the Western world does there exist one dominant religious culture.

2. _____ points to different interpretive frameworks that support a variety of conclusions concerning fundamental issues of life and truth.
    a) Modern pluralism
    b) Theological pluralism

c) Religious skepticism

d) Radical skepticism

3. One consequence of modern pluralism is that people are reluctant to commit to any one religious position, which in turn creates a tendency toward one or more position(s). What is/are those position(s)?

a) Theological pluralism

b) Religious skepticism

c) Universal skepticism

d) A & B

e) B & C

f) All of the above

4. (T/F) The theological pluralist is being tolerant by asserting that all religions are wrong to claim exclusivity.

5. (T/F) From the outset, the gospel was proclaimed as both an exclusive all-inclusive message in that while Jesus is the only way to salvation, the salvation made possible through him is available to all people.

6. The belief "that each person has a unique core of feeling and intuition that should unfold or be expressed if individuality is to be realized" is called what?

a) Theological pluralism

b) Religious skepticism

c) Expressive individualism

d) Self-authorizing morality

7. Which belief holds personal choice as the highest good?

a) Radical nihilism

b) Modern pluralism

c) Expressive individualism

d) Self-authorizing morality

8. What thing(s) does the late modern credo "turn to the self" lack?

a) Grounding

b) Motivation

c) Hope
d) All of the above

9. (T/F) Our culture's emphasis on authenticity is typically just code for finding what new group you will join.

10. Christianity says that humans find _____ difficult, if not impossible, because we have been hard-wired by God to live with purpose and meaning.

a) Skepticism
b) Nihilism
c) Pluralism
d) Secularism

CHAPTER 12

Dealing with Defeaters

You Should Know

- Doing apologetics is like drawing a map for a person. Each person needs a specific map tailored to them; in the same way, apologists must craft their responses to the person they are engaging.

- There are many defeaters that people level against Christianity. In this section, eight of the most common are discussed.

- The *inside out* approach can be applied to each defeater as the authors provide a trajectory for future apologetic conversations.

- Christianity has an ample amount of resources to adequately respond to all of the defeaters in this section. In the end, Christianity tells a better story.

- A significant point often overlooked in street-level discussion about homosexuality is that both Jesus and Paul appeal to the creation order when discussing marriage.

- "Following your heart": An assumption of expressive individualism that people are to look within themselves to find their true self is impractical.

- The experiential problem of evil: how people understand and deal with bad things that happen in their own lives

- The secular optimistic take: There is no transcendent meaning in the world that we can discover; we are left to create our own meaning.

Reflection Questions

1. Describe the common view that Christianity takes the fun out of life. How might we respond to this objection?

2. In what ways does Christianity liberate people?

3. Explain why secularists have no clear basis from which to judge something as good or evil.

Discussion Question

1. Utilizing the two-step approach, outline how to respond to criticisms concerning slavery and segregation. Include the four biblical dynamics that were driving forces in the desegregation movement.

Quiz

1. The credo "just following your heart" assumes _____.
   a) Religious lethargy
   b) Self-authorizing morality
   c) Expressive individualism
   d) Theological pluralism

2. (T/F) Perhaps the most acute problem with self-authorizing morality is its impracticality.

3. Both Jesus and Paul appeal to the _____ when discussing marriage.
   a) Natural law
   b) Common sense
   c) Creation order
   d) Mosaic code

4. Which is NOT one of the points regarding the failure of individual Christians to live up to Christianity's high standards of virtue?
   a) The church has committed numerous sins throughout the years (e.g., slavery and segregation), but this doesn't necessarily disprove Christianity
   b) Just because someone who claims to be a Christian does something bad, it doesn't mean Christianity is bad

c) According to Christian theology, individual Christian growth takes place over time

d) Sometimes people convert to Christianity out of abusive or other unstable, dysfunctional situations

5. (T/F) The two-step approach for answering critiques of the church's failures involves 1) admitting past failures and 2) correcting and clarifying the prevailing anti-Christian narrative.

6. The initial problem with _____ is that the central claim it makes—that science is the only criteria for discovering truth—cannot be justified by science and therefore undermines itself.

a) Science
b) Scientism
c) Secularism
d) Naturalism

7. The problem with a "_____" is that secularism actually has its own set of beliefs and values that cannot be proven and therefore requires a type of faith.

a) Division telling
b) Deduction story
c) False narrative
d) Subtraction story

8. Which of the following is a common response to the defeater argument often connected to a "coming-of-age narrative" prevalent in today's culture?

a) "Faith, in contrast to reason and science, is for people who believe things without any evidence"

b) "Christians are a bunch of hypocrites; this includes many of the individuals I meet today and the way the church has collectively mistreated people through history"

c) "The Christian sexual ethic is dehumanizing, and Christians are homophobic"

d) "Christianity is too restrictive. It denies people the opportunity to flourish by following their heart"

9. Which is a point used to challenge the moralistic religious take on suffering?

   a) Christianity does not glorify suffering as something to seek out or to face with stoic indifference
   b) Christianity does not teach that there is some sort of simple cause-and-effect relationship between sin and suffering
   c) Christianity does not teach that evil is an illusion or that we should seek to overcome suffering by detaching ourselves from the world around us
   d) The Christian God gives humans real choices and responsibilities, but he is at the same time the ultimate sovereign and his divine plan cannot be thwarted

10. (T/F) Secularists have no clear basis from which to judge something as good or evil.

CHAPTER 13

Making a Case

You Should Know

- Christian persuasion should be holistic.

- Christian apologists can use the signposts of life as a means of pointing to a transcendent reality beyond the material world.

- The Christian story answers the deep questions of life that every person seeks to answer.

- The death and resurrection of Jesus is the central part of the Christian story.

- Christians have good historical evidence to believe the resurrection happened. Five hundred plus saw the resurrected Jesus, and some of them were skeptical prior to seeing him. The early disciples would have had little to gain and much to lose by advocating an unpopular story.

- While apologetics should be contextual, it should also be formed out of the right context.

- The wisdom of the cross, so central in drawing the right apologetic map for the right situation, grows within the rich soil of God's people singing, reading, feasting, praying, and confessing around God's Word.

- The different meanings for *morality* when discussing the relationship between morality and science: morality is used to mean the realm of right and wrong; morality is used to mean the social rules and practices of a given society at a purely descriptive level; morality is used to mean something that is more practical or instrumental.

- From a naturalistic perspective, there is no reason to suppose content generated by neurological structures is true.

- Moral realism: Morality exists independently of our perception or feelings.

Reflection Questions

1. Is it possible to "do away with value judgments altogether"? Why or why not?

2. Summarize the three possible meanings science has for morality.

3. Why was the worship of a crucified and resurrected Messiah scandalous in the first-century world?

Discussion Question

1. How can Christians tell "the greatest story ever told" as the true answer to life's universal questions? Explain that story.

Quiz

1. _____ is concerned with the way we behave rather than the truthfulness of our beliefs.
    a) Survivalistic evolution
    b) Theistic evolution
    c) Naturalistic evolution
    d) Rationalistic evolution

2. (T/F) Materialists consider the fine-tuning argument persuasive.

3. Even if one refuses to assent intellectually to _____, people find moral judgments to be irresistible in practice.
    a) Moral idealism
    b) Moral rationalism
    c) Moral realism
    d) Moral relativism

4. Many _____ will argue that all value judgments are illusory and determined by cultural conditioning.

    a) Culturalists

    b) Materialists

    c) Moral realists

    d) Environmentalists

5. Which is NOT one of the possible meanings for morality when discussing its relationship with science?

    a) Morality is used to mean that which is plausible

    b) Morality is used to mean the realm of right and wrong

    c) Morality is used to mean the social rules and practices of a given society at a purely descriptive level

    d) Morality is used to mean something that is more practical or instrumental

6. (T/F) Science does not provide moral obligation.

7. The eighteenth-century skeptic _____ claimed that one could never be confident in the actual occurrence of a miracle because a miracle would violate the laws of nature.

    a) Adam Smith

    b) David Hume

    c) Immanuel Kant

    d) René Descartes

8. Within a first-century context, _____ were not believed to give trustworthy testimony on important matters and were not allowed to testify in a court of law.

    a) Gentiles

    b) Samaritans

    c) Moabites

    d) Women

9. (T/F) If the resurrection was a hoax, it would have been counter-intuitive for the story to have begun in Jerusalem because that's where Jesus died and was buried.

10. The worship of a crucified and resurrected Messiah was scandalous in the first-century world because it was blasphemy for _____ to worship a human.

    a) Jews
    b) Greeks
    c) Samaritans
    d) Women

Notes

www.ingramcontent.com/pod-product-compliance
Lightning Source LLC
Chambersburg PA
CBHW010921040426
42445CB00017B/1938